SCHIRMER'S LIBRARY OF MUSICAL CLASSICS

Vol. 1278

Johann Sebastian Bach

Six Suites

Originally written for Violoncello Solo

Adapted, Revised
and Fingered for

VIOLA

By

Louis Svećenski

G. SCHIRMER, Inc.

DISTRIBUTED BY

Hal•Leonard®

Copyright, 1916, by G. Schirmer, Inc.
Copyright renewed, 1944, by G. Schirmer, Inc.

Visit Hal Leonard Online at
www.halleonard.com

Contact us:
Hal Leonard
7777 West Bluemound Road
Milwaukee, WI 53213
Email: info@halleonard.com

In Europe, contact:
Hal Leonard Europe Limited
42 Wigmore Street
Marylebone, London, W1U 2RN
Email: info@halleonardeurope.com

In Australia, contact:
Hal Leonard Australia Pty. Ltd.
4 Lentara Court
Cheltenham, Victoria, 3192 Australia
Email: info@halleonard.com.au

Explanation of Marks

I = A-String
II = D "
III = G "
IV = C "

W = whole bow
U = upper }
M = middle } part of bow
L = lower }

– – – – } notes to be detached,
– – – – } but not in staccato manner.

– on single note means that same should be held a trifle longer than its actual value *(tenuto)*.

notes to be well separated

The dot outside of the slur indicates that the note should be given a trifle less than its actual value. It is to be slurred with the preceding note of the group, and ended lightly.

1_____ The line following a finger-mark indicates how long the fingers should retain their places.

, = Very slight pause (breathing pause), to separate phrases.

Suite I

J. S. Bach
Adapted, revised and fingered
for Viola by
Louis Svečenski

Prélude
Allegro moderato (quasi andante)

6

Allemande
Molto moderato

Courante
Allegro non troppo

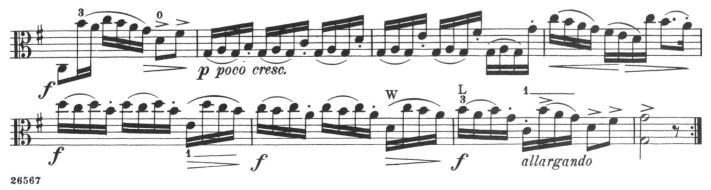

26567

8

Sarabande
Lento

Menuetto I
Moderato

Menuetto II

Gigue
Allegro vivo

Suite II

Prélude
Allegro moderato

Allemande
Molto moderato

Courante
Allegro non troppo

Sarabande
Lento

Menuetto I
Moderato

Menuetto II

Gigue
Vivace

Suite III

Prélude
Allegro moderato

Allemande

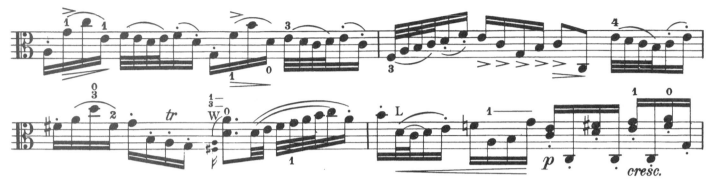

26567

Courante

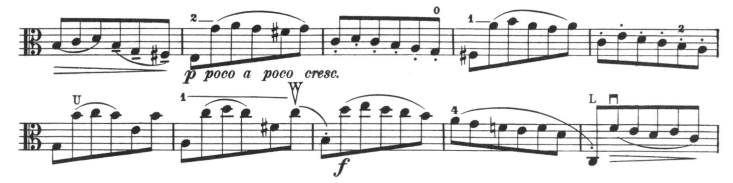

26567

Sarabande

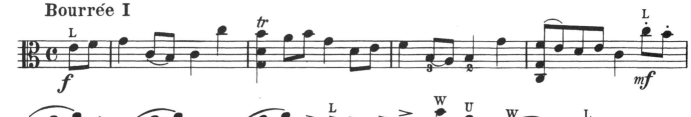

Bourrée I

Bourrée II

Bourrée I D.C.

Gigue

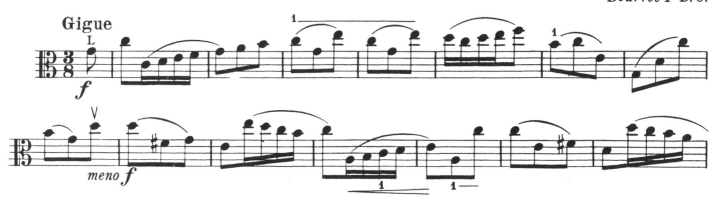

26567

Suite IV

Prélude

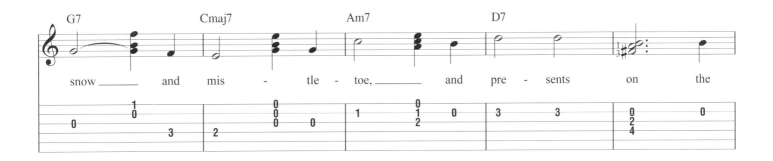

snow _____ and mis - tle - toe, _____ and pre - sents on the

tree. _____ Christ - mas Eve will find me _____

_____ where the love - light gleams. _____

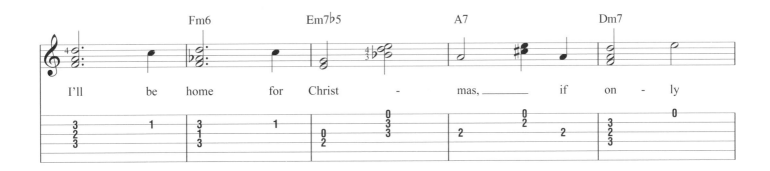

I'll be home for Christ - mas, _____ if on - ly

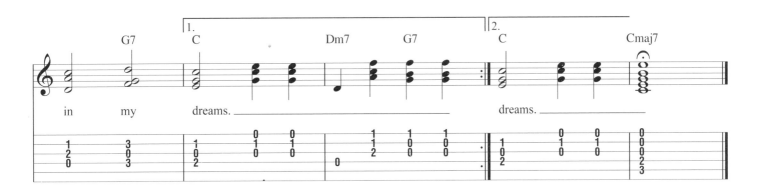

in my dreams. _____ dreams. _____

Jingle Bell Rock

Words and Music by Joe Beal and Jim Boothe

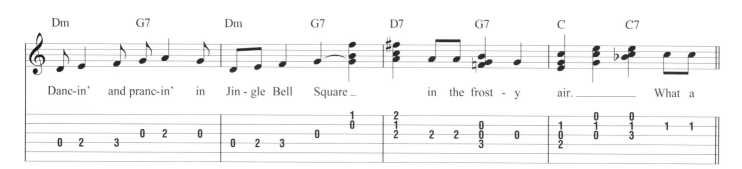

bright time, it's the right time to rock the night a-way.____ Jin-gle

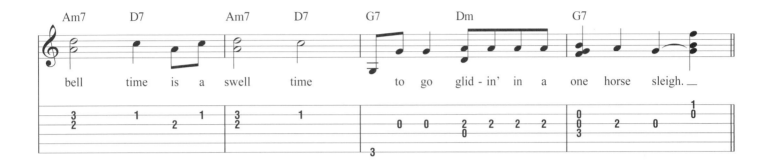

bell time is a swell time to go glid-in' in a one horse sleigh.__

Outro

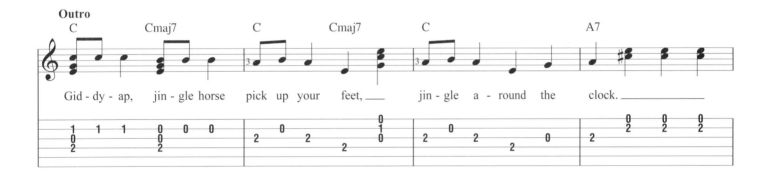

Gid-dy-ap, jin-gle horse pick up your feet,___ jin-gle a-round the clock.____

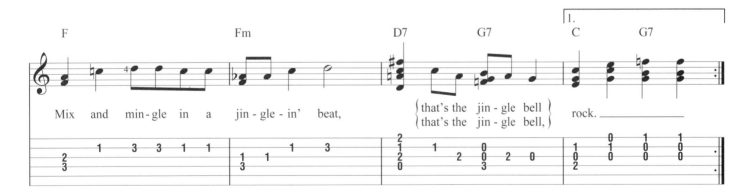

Mix and min-gle in a jin-gle-in' beat, { that's the jin-gle bell } rock.____

{ that's the jin-gle bell, }

that's the jin-gle bell, that's the jin-gle bell rock.____

Last Christmas

Words and Music by George Michael

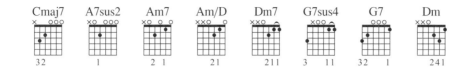

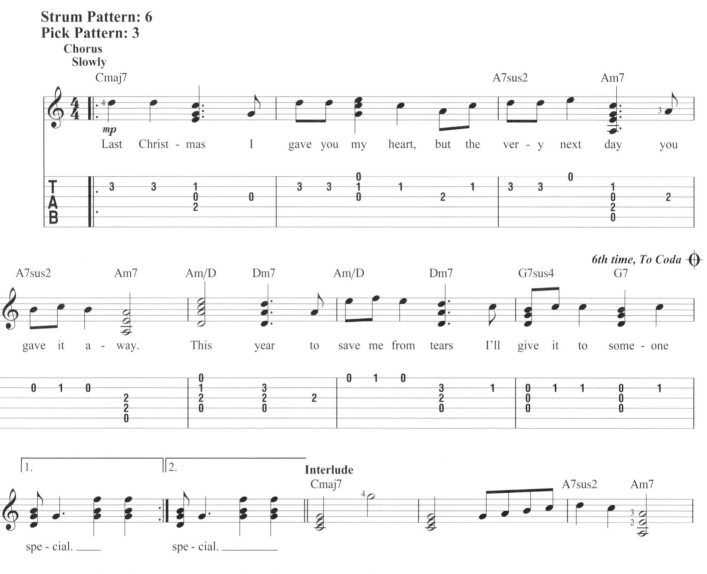

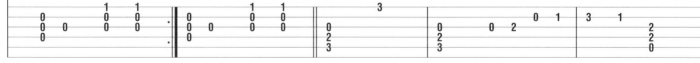

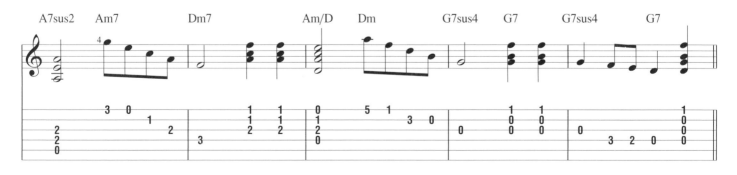

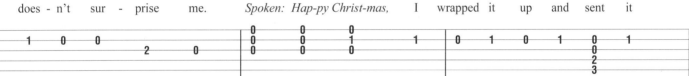

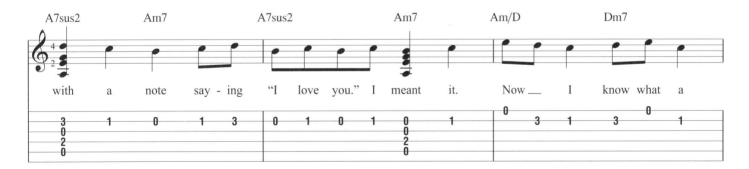

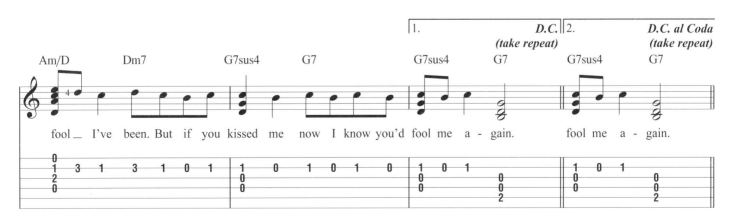

Additional Lyrics

A crowded room, friends with tired eyes.
I'm hiding from you and your soul of ice.
My God, I thought you were someone to rely on.
Me, I guess I was a shoulder to cry on.
A face on a lover with a fire in his heart,
A man undercover but you tore me apart,
Ooh, now I've found a real love.
You'll never fool me again.

Merry Christmas, Darling

Words and Music by Richard Carpenter and Frank Pooler

Strum Pattern: 4
Pick Pattern: 4

Suite V

Prélude
Adagio

Allegro moderato

poco a poco cresc.

f

meno f

cresc.

f sempre

dim.

mp

cresc.

Allemande

Corrente

Sarabande

Gavotte I

Gavotte II

Gigue

Suite VI

Prélude

Allemande

mf molto espr.

mp

p

mf *p*

p

tr *cresc.*

mf

ten. *mf* *mf*

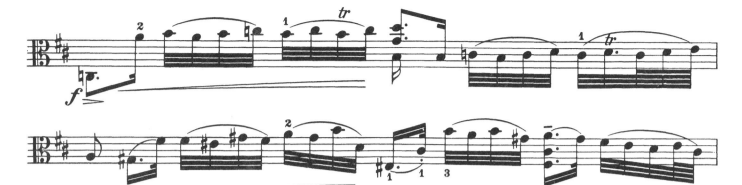

Corrente

50

Sarabande *)

Gavotte I

*) The original key of this Sarabande is D major, in which it is impracticable for the Viola; therefore it has been transposed to G major.

26567

Gavotte II

Gigue